A25257

Charles Dickens

Nigel Hunter

Illustrations by Edward Mortelmans

Great Lives

Beethoven
Louis Braille
Julius Caesar
Winston Churchill
Captain Cook
Marie Curie
Charles Dickens
Francis Drake
Einstein
Queen Elizabeth I
Queen Elizabeth II
Anne Frank
Gandhi
Henry VIII
Joan of Arc

Helen Keller
John F. Kennedy
Martin Luther King
Mary, Queen of Scots
John Lennon
Ferdinand Magellan
Karl Marx
Mozart
Napoleon
Florence Nightingale
Elvis Presley
William Shakespeare
Tchaikovsky
Mother Teresa
Queen Victoria

All the words that appear in **bold** are explained in the glossary on page 31.

Editor: Marcella Streets

First published in 1988 by
Wayland (Publishers) Limited
61 Western Road, Hove
East Sussex BN3 1JD, England

© Copyright 1988 Wayland (Publishers) Limited

British Library Cataloguing in Publication Data
Hunter, Nigel
   Charles, Dickens.
   1. Fiction in English. Dickens, Charles
   1812–1870 – Biographies
   I. Title   II. Series
   823′.8

   ISBN 1–85210–182–2

Phototypeset by Kalligraphics Ltd, Redhill, Surrey
Printed in Italy by G. Canale & C.S.p.A., Turin
Bound in France by AGM

Contents

Face to face

The great public hall was packed full, with the audience waiting expectantly. Then there was a wave of excitement, and thunderous cheering. Charles Dickens stepped on to the platform and then strode purposefully across to the reading desk.

For the next three hours his listeners sat entranced. One by one, familiar characters from his books seemed miraculously to come alive as he acted out their parts in the story. Sometimes, people said, one side of his face seemed one character, the other side another.

He knew how to tell his stories to the utmost effect. He could tease out their humour until people were laughing fit to burst. With the murder of Nancy from *Oliver Twist*, he could have the audience writhing with horror; with the death of little Paul

Right *Dickens' public readings held his audience spellbound.*

Insert *The tragic character of Paul from* Dombey and Son.

Dombey, people broke down and wept unashamedly.

Dickens was perhaps the most popular writer of Victorian England. For the whole of his 35-year career, his books had a vast

and faithful following. By the end of his life, he had created a whole fictional 'world', teeming with hundreds of memorable characters.

It was a world of flickering light and dark shadows, sometimes a menacing world. For his novels not only entertained, they also dealt with many pressing problems of the time. During his lifetime Dickens became well known as a **social reformist**.

He was a very energetic man, generous and sociable, with a large family and many close friends. His public adored him; but only two people knew the secret agony of his childhood.

Nursery stories

Charles Dickens was born at Portsea, near Portsmouth, in 1812. His father, John Dickens, was a Royal Navy pay clerk, who tended to spend his own money rather too freely. It was hard, sometimes, to meet the household bills. Soon the family had to move to a smaller, cheaper home.

Two years later they moved again, to London; and two years after that, to Chatham, on the **estuary** of the River Thames.

Here Dickens spent his happiest years.

It was his nursemaid, Mary Weller, who first sparked his imagination with stories. Her spine-chilling, gory tales of ghosts and ferocious murders kept him awake at night but he enjoyed them greatly.

However, it was his mother, Elizabeth Dickens, who taught him to read. He always remained

Young Charles revelled in his nursemaid's blood-curdling stories!

especially grateful to her for that. He read and re-read all the fairy tales he could find. 'Little Red Riding Hood was my first love,' he once declared.

Soon he discovered the stories of *The Arabian Nights,* and later classic novels like *Peregrine Pickle, Don Quixote* and *Robinson Crusoe.* All of them contributed to the kind of books he would one day write himself.

Charles and his elder sister Fanny were talented performers of comic songs. They even made public appearances, standing on tables at a local hotel, singing for their father's friends! For the

Magic lantern shows were popular in Victorian Britain.

family, they also put on **magic lantern** shows, and spirited theatrical dramas.

Dickens was fascinated by the theatre – by pantomimes, circuses, and plays of all sorts. He also enjoyed the noisy bustle of the quaysides and streets of Chatham, and the ancient, peaceful surroundings of nearby Rochester Cathedral.

But not far off lay an altogether harsher, crueller world: before long, Chatham would seem only a distant dream.

7

Hope and despair

Charles and Fanny went to two small schools in Chatham. The fearsome old lady who ran the first school they attended, used to rap Charles's head with her knuckles to make him pay attention! However, their second teacher recognized both children's talents.

One day, while Charles was out walking with his father, they came within sight of a beautiful ivy-clad house, with great bow windows, a white-columned doorway, and spacious gardens. There was even a small bell tower on the roof. This was Gad's Hill Place.

Some day, his father told him, if he worked hard, he might live in a house like that – perhaps in that very same one. Charles was never to forget it.

Meanwhile his father's free-spending habits had begun to cause serious concern. Late in 1822, John Dickens' employers transferred him to London. After finishing the school term, Charles joined his family.

Poverty was tightening its grip on the growing family: after a year, they had nothing left to **pawn**. Though Fanny went to the Royal Academy of Music, Charles's own education seemed finished. As he turned twelve, in 1824, he was sent to work.

For 12 hours a day he laboured in Warren's **blacking** warehouse down by the river. It was a filthy, half-rotten, rat-infested place, and the work was sheer drudgery: tying paper round pots of blacking-paste, then

Gad's Hill Place, near Chatham – the house that Dickens admired as a boy, and eventually bought in 1856.

gluing on the labels. His high hopes plunged.

Worse still, his father had been arrested – and his mother and the four younger children had gone to live with him in Marshalsea debtors' prison. Charles and Fanny visited them at weekends. Meanwhile Charles lived alone in cheap lodgings, eking out his pennies day by day.

Charles's few months in the boot-blacking factory were the most miserable of his life.

His miserable situation lasted only a few months, but the impression it left on him was life-long. The ordeals of many outcast children in his books showed how deeply he was scarred.

9

London life

Luckily, John Dickens inherited enough money to pay off his debts and secure his release from prison. One day, he happened to glance through a window and saw his son toiling away. It seemed such a pitiful sight that he decided 'the young gentleman' (as Charles's equally young workmates called him) should be allowed to resume his schooling. For the next three years, Dickens attended the Wellington House Academy.

He began to put the recent past behind him – only once afterwards did he ever refer to it.

Charles's schoolfellows found him bright, outgoing, and fun to be with. He wrote thrilling, chilling stories to read aloud. He acted in school plays, and put on miniature dramas in toy theatres. But he was unimpressed by the school's general standards: he later said its Head was 'by far the most ignorant man' he had ever had the pleasure to know!

At fifteen, Charles began work in a law office. It was a dull routine, with masses of seemingly pointless paperwork. His ambitions went much further. Having worked hard to learn shorthand, he became a **freelance** reporter in the Law Courts.

He was also getting to know the varied life of London's streets, from the smart buildings of the new West End to the slums and damp alleyways of its poorest

quarters. He visited theatres constantly, seeing all the most popular shows. At 'private' theatres, where people could pay to perform, he sometimes went on stage himself.

Soon after his twentieth birthday, he became a parliamentary reporter. It was so cramped in the old House of Lords that the reporters had to write standing up, 'huddled together like so many sheep'. His reports of the politicians' speeches were almost word-perfect. But Dickens considered most Members of Parliament 'clowns'. It was an opinion events did nothing to change.

Charles began to develop his story-telling talents at school.

Enter 'Boz'

At the same time as he was making his mark as a young reporter, Charles Dickens fell desperately in love with the beautiful Maria Beadnell. At first, all went well. He was a regular guest at her family's musical evenings, displaying his own talents to the full; he and Maria swapped many small tokens of affection.

Her parents seemed to think him an unsuitable match, however. Perhaps they had heard of his father's disgrace. They sent Maria abroad for some months and, when she returned, for some reason she was cold towards him. Hard as he tried, he failed to regain her love. He felt bitter and humiliated, as well as heartbroken, and suffered the memory of it for many years.

In the late autumn of 1833, Dickens dropped a short piece of writing into the office of the *Monthly Magazine*. It was an amusing **sketch** of London life called 'A Dinner at Poplar Walk',

Dickens' love for Maria Beadnell was discouraged by her father.

The hopeful young author submits his first comic sketch.

and it proved a great success. The editor asked for more and Dickens was happy to oblige.

At first his pieces appeared with no name attached. But to the fifth, published the following summer, he fixed the signature 'Boz'. In years to come, he was to be known by this name throughout the English-speaking world.

Meanwhile, as the political correspondent of a daily newspaper, he continued his reporting career. He travelled to far-flung parts of the country, covering meetings and elections. Rushing back in the coach overnight, writing all the way, he tried hard to be first with the news.

Then he met George Hogarth, editor of the *Evening Chronicle* – and his daughter, Kate. The paper published many more of his sketches, among them 'Gin Shops', 'Public Dinners', 'Our Parish' and 'The Pawnbroker's Shop'. Before long, there were plans to publish them in book form. Charles and Kate also had plans concerning each other.

Kate Hogarth soon became the focus of Charles's attention.

Rising high

With the success of his early writings, Dickens became something of a 'dandy' — a stylishly-dressed man-about-town. He was getting to know many of London's leading literary people, and could well afford to think of marriage.

His first book, *Sketches by Boz*, came out in two volumes in February 1836, with sixteen sharply-drawn, witty illustrations by the great George Cruickshank. A reviewer called it 'the merriest book of the season'. But it also contained serious **social comment**: one piece described a grim visit Dickens had made to the **notorious** Newgate Prison.

He and Kate Hogarth were married that spring. With them in their home lived Charles's younger brother Fred, and Kate's fifteen-year-old sister Mary. It was not an unusual arrangement in those days.

Charles Dickens quickly became a central figure in London's literary scene.

Many people who liked to read in Dickens' times were unable to afford books. However, they could afford a regular magazine, in which novels were published in **instalments**; and Dickens' new story, *The Posthumous Papers of the Pickwick Club*, was causing a sensation.

All over the country, month by month, people were following the adventures of its main characters, Mr Pickwick and his sharp-witted young servant, Sam Weller. Like nearly all Dickens' work in the future, it was

Prison made even the normally cheerful Mr Pickwick feel downhearted.

illustrated by Hablôt Knight Browne – better known as 'Phiz'. Its author signed himself 'Boz the Magnificent'!

Much in demand, he wrote a play and an **operatic libretto**, and became the editor of a new magazine. Then, even before 'Pickwick' was finished, he began another novel – the tale of an orphan adrift in London's criminal underworld. Its title was *Oliver Twist*.

Victims

Oliver Twist showed the depth of Dickens' concern for society's victims. Its most memorable scene pictured Oliver at supper in the poor boys' workhouse, pathetically asking for 'more'.

Just as the first chapters were written, Dickens' first son was born. Then suddenly, his sister-in-law Mary died. He was devastated. 'I knew her inmost heart,' he wrote, 'she had not a fault.'

In the January snows of 1838, Dickens and Phiz went to Yorkshire. Charles was already planning his next novel, and wanted to visit certain boarding schools, where he had heard conditions were grim. At one alone, he noticed 25 graves. Soon afterwards he began *Nicholas Nickleby* – with half of *Oliver Twist* still to complete.

Each instalment left the public eager to know what would happen next. When each story was finished, it was published as a book. Sales were huge. People of all ages and backgrounds enjoyed them: families read them aloud, and the young Queen Victoria praised them to her Prime Minister.

With two more babies now – both daughters – Dickens and his wife moved to a fine new house near Regent's Park, London. Here, he entertained friends lavishly. The family also enjoyed visiting the Kent seaside resort of

Nicholas Nickleby told of horrific school conditions.

Broadstairs. He bought a country cottage for his parents.

Charles's next venture was a new **journal**, *Master Humphrey's Clock*. In it he published *The Old Curiosity Shop*, with its famous heart-rending ending, the death of Little Nell. Writing it, he re-lived the tragedy of Mary's death – and many readers mourned Nell almost as badly.

Then came *Barnaby Rudge*, a historical novel about riots and revolt. Dickens feared and despised violence. He wanted the world to change for the better, but in a peaceful way.

Mary Hogarth's sad death was a devastating blow for Dickens.

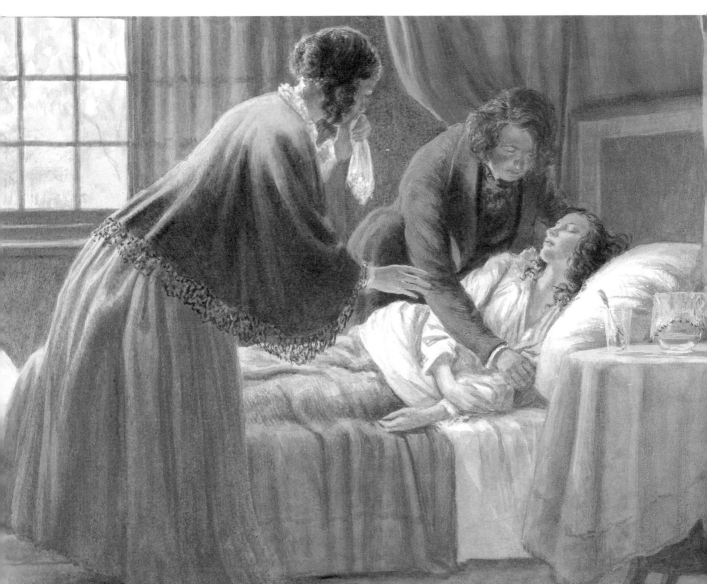

The USA

Shortly before his thirtieth birthday, Dickens set off with Kate for the USA, leaving the children in the care of close family friends – the great actor William Macready and his wife. They sailed in one of the first ocean-going steamships, meeting a terrible storm midway, and nearly being wrecked off Nova Scotia. But finally they reached Boston.

The moment they docked, excited newspaper reporters leapt aboard for interviews. It seemed everyone wanted to meet Dickens. There were dozens of dinner invitations; crowds gathered at his hotel, and when he went out, people lined the streets and cheered.

Charles went to the theatre to see a show featuring scenes from his books, and was applauded wildly. The city threw a grand welcoming ball for him. As he signed autographs at breakfast, a painter sketched his portrait, while a sculptor modelled him in clay. As one admirer said: 'There never was, and never will be, such a triumph.'

Dickens visited cotton mills, asylums for the insane and schools for the blind, finding conditions generally much better than in Britain. But as the tour continued, he became weary of the constant public attention. Hundreds of strangers lined up to shake his hand; others pulled fur from his coat for a souvenir.

Also, serious arguments broke out between Dickens and the

American press over the fact that they printed foreign books without paying the authors. He was shocked, too, by what he saw of slavery and made his feelings quite clear in *American Notes*. He was also sickened by men continually spitting filthy streams of tobacco-juice: even the President had a **spittoon**!

However he became good friends with several famous authors, including Henry Longfellow, Washington Irving and Edgar Allen Poe, and he found Niagara Falls impressive.

Altogether though, the USA had disappointed him. After six months, he and Kate were glad to be home, reunited with their children.

Dickens was disgusted by the sale of black people as slaves.

Good causes

Dickens' *American Notes* included some blunt criticisms of the USA, which many Americans found offensive. Even close friends thought certain parts unreasonably hostile. Many people read it, nonetheless.

To boost sales of his next novel, *Martin Chuzzlewit*, he wrote a section giving his hero some American adventures and found himself laughing uncontrollably at his own sarcasm and wit. But the book's humour bit sharply – his American readers, he said, had gone 'stark staring raving mad' over it!

In Dickens' time, some poor children were sold by their parents as chimney sweeps.

He considered this his best novel so far. Its story of greed and selfishness reflected some of his deepest concerns about society. The gap between rich and poor people seemed to him to be ever-widening.

Dickens frequently spoke at fund-raising dinners on behalf of good causes, including hospitals and welfare societies, and he organized support for the families of friends who had died, or fallen on hard times.

Then he became involved with what were known as the Ragged Schools of London's slums. The teachers worked hard to educate their poor pupils, in often overcrowded and filthy conditions. Dickens described the schools as being 'like an ugly dream'. He urged a generous friend, the banking heiress

Dickens asked Baroness Coutts to help improve the Ragged Schools.

Baroness Angela Coutts, to help provide better facilities, as he believed education was vital.

The plight of **impoverished** children gave rise to one of his most popular tales, *A Christmas Carol*. A ghost story and a humorous **moral fable**, it told of an unfeeling miser converted to goodness. One of his friends commented that, to everyone who read it, Dickens had done 'a personal kindness'.

He and his family and friends celebrated Christmas that year with crazy, fun-filled parties. One guest declared him 'the *best* conjuror' she had ever seen! Another of Kate's young sisters, Georgina Hogarth, was part of the family now, and Charles and Kate's fifth child was expected in the New Year.

Italy

In the summer of 1844, the whole family – with three maids, a French **courier**, and their dog, Timber – set off for Italy. They travelled through France in a 'good old shabby devil of a coach' Dickens had bought, then sailed from Marseilles to the city of Genoa in northern Italy.

At first they rented a great gaunt old villa there, which he called the 'Pink Gaol'. Later, they moved to the magnificent 'Palace of the Fishponds', with its terraces, groves of fruit trees, and its seven fountains.

Dickens relaxed contentedly in Italy's warm climate, swimming in the bay, and learning to speak Italian. One day, in Genoa's backstreets, he came across a puppet theatre: the little figures' antics amused him greatly.

In Italy, Dickens wrote his second 'Christmas Book', *The Chimes*, which was meant as 'a great blow for the poor', he said. He made a quick visit to London to read it to some of his closest friends. 'There was not a dry eye in the house,' he reported happily to Kate. He was well known in Europe by now. Returning to Italy through Paris, he met other notable writers including Victor Hugo and Alexandre Dumas.

Dickens saw much of Italy during his stay, visiting several northern cities prior to his London trip, and journeying southward after his return. The ancient majesty of cities such as Venice and Rome struck him as glorious, but he felt oppressed by the strong religious feeling. However, he liked the people very much, and many sights, like Pompeii and Vesuvius, were unforgettable. Climbing through snow to the flaming tip of the volcano, he peered over the edge of the crater to view the lava bubbling and hissing inside.

In Italy he also put to use his longtime interest in **hypnosis**. He hypnotized a new friend, Madame De la Rue, hoping to cure her of a nervous disease. But their sessions together led to some jealousy on Kate's part. It was the first hint of a strain in their marriage, and after their return to England, Dickens seemed more and more restless.

Dickens and his family enjoyed Italy's colourful street life.

Public and private

In the late 1840s, Dickens became involved in many new projects.

He formed an amateur acting company out of his circle of friends, and they put on plays – mostly comedies – in aid of various causes. He organized everything from costumes to

Dickens was a fine actor. In 1848 he played Sir Charles Coldstream in the play, Used Up.

stage-sets, and acted and directed too. Most performances were public, but some were rather exclusive: twice they appeared especially for Queen Victoria and Prince Albert.

For a short time, Dickens became editor of a daily paper which called for 'progress, education and **liberty**'. Among other articles, he wrote a strong attack on **capital punishment**. The paper also published his *Pictures from Italy*.

Dickens spent a further six months abroad with his family, mostly at Lausanne in Switzerland. Back in London, he became closely involved in setting up and running a refuge for 'fallen women' with Angela Coutts. There, he hoped, female **prostitutes** could gain the chance of a new life.

He wrote three more 'Christmas' books and two further novels. *Dombey and Son* concerned a hard-headed businessman, and his son and daughter. Its story dealt with the battle between business values and human values.

Then Dickens wrote *David Copperfield* which grew out of thoughts about his own childhood. It was a mixture of truth and **fiction**, he told his closest friend, John Forster. In the book, David's love for Dora echoed Dickens' old love for Maria Beadnell.

He also wrote a private account of his time in the blacking factory, which he showed only to Forster and Kate. It remained a

The treacherous Uriah Heep wrings his bony hands as he grovels to the young David Copperfield.

secret from the public during the whole of his lifetime.

Then in 1850 he launched a new magazine called *Household Words*. It set out both to entertain and inform its readers, and quickly became a great popular success.

The 1850s

Dickens wrote *A Child's History of England* with his own children in mind. Tragically, soon after starting it, his baby Dora died. His father had also died, just a few weeks previously. In 1853 Kate gave birth to their last child, a boy he nicknamed 'Plorn' (short for 'Mr Plornishmaroontigoonter'!).

His novels of the 1850s became increasingly critical of Victorian society. His powers of expression were at their peak.

In *Bleak House*, he blasted the tiresome confusion of the Law, suggesting society was **corrupt** and an obstacle to human happiness. *Hard Times* was set in a mill town. It concentrated on school life and factory life, and the harsh outlook of mill owners. *Little Dorrit* was set largely in the place where his father had been gaoled. It suggested that society made everyone a 'prisoner' in some way or other.

The Dickens' family home was now a grand, 18-room mansion.

Dickens' pet raven inspired several stories in his magazine.

Dickens' friend Wilkie Collins, author of The Moonstone.

They still spent long periods abroad. Boulogne, in northern France, was a favourite summer resort. They also lived for five months in Paris.

Among the contributors to *Household Words* were several new writers Dickens admired, including Elizabeth Gaskell and Wilkie Collins. With Collins, he became firm friends. They went on a jaunt to Italy, and enjoyed exploring the sleazy parts of London and Paris together.

Dickens' acting company appeared triumphantly in many cities. He also began to give public readings from his books for charity at Christmas.

When his first lost love, Maria Beadnell, wrote to him, he was eager to meet her again. However, when he did, unexpectedly, he found her quite similar to his wife. Over the years, he and Kate had grown further and further apart.

A playbill advertising a charity performance by Dickens' acting company in 1852.

Final fruits

Dickens' separation from Kate in 1858 was a bitter affair. There were hints of scandal, as London literary society gossiped about his friendship with a young actress, Ellen Ternan. Dickens made matters worse by denying the truth of these rumours in a statement to the papers.

The outcome was that Kate occupied one house while he lived in another. Their eldest son lived with her; the others lived with him and their Aunt Georgy (Kate's sister). Dickens had just bought Gad's Hill Place – the house he had known and longed for as a boy.

He launched a magazine called *All the Year Round* and here he published *A Tale of Two Cities*, a novel set in London and Paris during the French Revolution. Then came *Great Expectations*: Pip's painful growth to adulthood was based on Dickens' own life.

He earned a lot of money now from his famous public readings,

Pip and Magwitch in the sinister opening to Great Expectations.

Dicken's Dream, *painted by R W Buss, who died before completing it.*

touring for months at a time. People flocked to see him, and were astonished by his skilful, well-practised delivery.

Dickens spent much of his time with Ellen. Once, on their way back from a stay in France, they were involved in a train crash which killed ten people. He kept calm, and helped the injured, but was always nervous afterwards of train travel. His last completed novel, *Our Mutual Friend*, involved murder and a double identity. Its theme was wealth and corruption.

Despite worrying signs of heart trouble, Dickens continued his public reading tours. Once again, he visited the USA, receiving rapturous acclaim. He drove himself on to the point of exhaustion, however. Finally, his doctors warned him to stop.

It was already too late, however. After a farewell tour, and an **audience** with Queen Victoria, he died on 9 June 1870 at the age of fifty-eight. *The Mystery of Edwin Drood* was left unfinished, and unresolved. In Westminster Abbey, London, his grave was heaped high with flowers for months: the ordinary people's tribute to 'the Inimitible Boz'.

Important dates

1812   Born in Portsea, southern England, 7 February.

1816   Family moves to Chatham, Kent.

1823   Moves to Camden Town, London.

1824   Father imprisoned for debt; working in Warren's blacking warehouse.

1827   Becomes clerk at Ellis and Blackmore, solicitors.

1829–33   Law Court/parliamentary reporter; working for the *True Sun, Mirror of Parliament* and *Morning Chronicle*.

1833–5   Writing sketches of everyday life.

1836   *Sketches by Boz* published. Marriage to Catherine (Kate) Hogarth. Begins *The Pickwick Papers*.

1837   Begins *Oliver Twist*. First of ten children born. Death of Mary Hogarth.

1838   Begins *Nicholas Nickleby*.

1840   Begins *The Old Curiosity Shop*.

1841   Begins *Barnaby Rudge*.

1842   Visits USA; publishes *American Notes*.

1843   Begins *Martin Chuzzlewit;* writes *A Christmas Carol*.

1844–5   Living in Italy; forms amateur acting company.

1846   *Pictures from Italy* published; living in Switzerland and France; begins *Dombey and Son*.

1849   Begins *David Copperfield*.

1850   Becomes editor/part owner of magazine *Household Words*.

1851   Starts *A Child's History of England*; death of father and baby daughter; begins *Bleak House*.

1853   Six months in France, Switzerland and Italy; first charity reading; begins *Hard Times*.

1855–6   Begins *Little Dorrit*; living in Paris.

1858   Separates from his wife. First professional reading tour.

1859   Launches magazine *All the Year Round*; begins *A Tale of Two Cities*.

1860   Begins *Great Expectations*.

1861–3   Further reading tours.

1864   Begins *Our Mutual Friend*.

1865   Involved in rail disaster.

1867–9   Further reading tours, including tour in USA; begins *The Mystery of Edwin Drood*.

1870   Farewell readings; death, 9 June.

Glossary

Audience An interview with someone important.

Blacking Substance used to blacken shoes, metal etc.

Capital punishment Punishment by death.

Corrupt Rotten and evil.

Courier Someone who looks after tourists and their travel arrangements.

Estuary The mouth or lower part of a river which is affected by high tides.

Fiction A story that is not true but is imaginary.

Freelance Someone who does not get a regular wage but sells work to several employers.

Hypnosis A sleep-like state brought about by someone who can then control your mind and actions.

Impoverished Made poor.

Instalments Parts of a story which are published one at a time in a magazine or newspaper.

Journal A newspaper or magazine, or a daily record of events.

Liberty Freedom.

Magic lantern An early form of slide projector, using scenes painted on glass.

Moral fable A short story that teaches a lesson about how to behave.

Notorious Famous or well-known for something bad.

Operatic libretto The words written to go with an opera, which is a play sung to music.

Pawn To leave something, e.g. a watch, with a pawnbroker when you borrow money, to make sure you repay the loan.

Prostitute Someone who has sex with someone else for money.

Sketch A short play or piece of writing, often amusing.

Social comment Opinion on society.

Social reformist Someone who tries to change things that they believe are bad about society.

Spittoon A container for spitting into.

Books to read

As They Saw Them – Charles Dickens by Michael and Mollie Hardwick (Harrap, 1970)

Charles Dickens by L. du Garde Peach (Ladybird, 1965)

Charles Dickens by Michael St John Parker (Pitkin Pictorials, 1973)

Charles Dickens and his World by J. B. Priestley (Thames and Hudson, 1961)

Dickens in his Time by Ivor Brown (Nelson & Sons, 1963)

Index